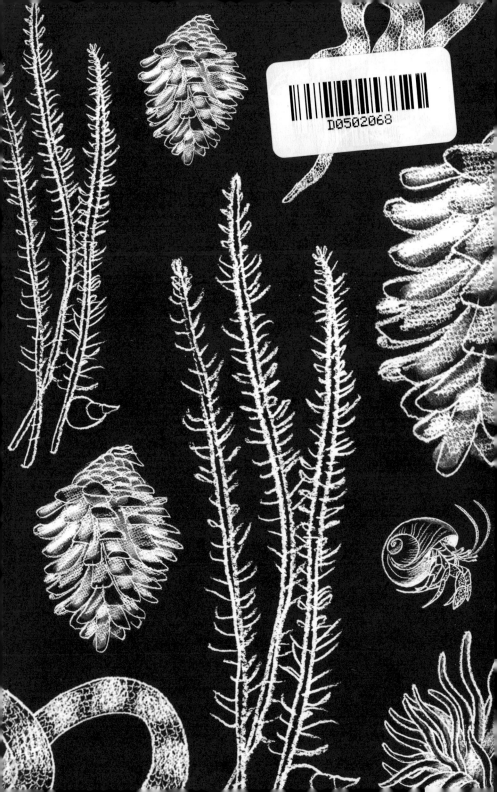

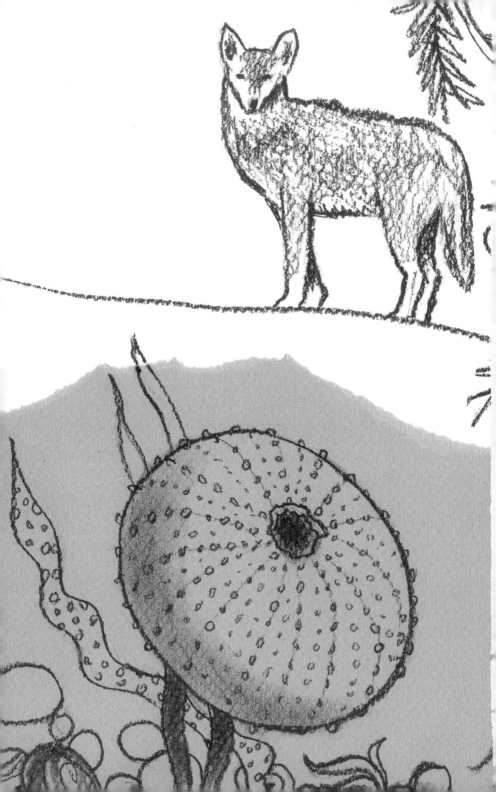

Nest, Nook & Cranny

Poems by Susan Blackaby

Illustrated by Jamie Hogan

Charlesbridge

Wetland

Woodland

Habitats

Writing Poetry

Before You Begin

habitat • the natural home of an animal or plant

The poems in this collection are loosely arranged by habitat, but you will find that coyotes, bugs, and birds (to name a few) don't give a hoot about labels. Thanks to accommodations or adaptations or both, some creatures can live anyplace. Keep that in mind when the boundaries blur.

My habitat is a woodland garden that used to be a dense rain forest. Fir, hemlock, and cedar boughs block the sunlight. Moss lines the pathways. Mist snags in the treetops. Showers soak into the roots of trees and shrubs.

Start under the shaggy cedar at the top of the bank. Follow the rivulets after a rain, and you will find where they trickle into the local pattern of creeks. The creeks meander to the river, which tumbles through oxbows and channels that lead, after a while, to the sea. Along the way you pass grassy pastures, with circling hawks and shy mice. You climb up and over the coast range. It is just high enough to keep the fog on the beach side of the mountains.

I share my habitat with many of the creatures whose homes are described in these poems. For one thing, I live in the beaver town (Beaverton) in the beaver state (Oregon). There are not as many beavers here as there were in the past, but you can still see them if you know where to look. Great blue herons fish in my neighbor's pond. Ducks and geese sweep low over the rooftops. Coyotes saunter up the street and disappear into the woods.

In my garden I have a little hut. It is where I go when I need quiet. It is a good place for thinking, for teasing out rhymes, for stringing words into images and ideas. It is a dry spot where an ancient rain forest once stood.

This is my habitat. What's yours?

Desert

Some animals are homebodies,
Like tortoises and snails.
Their heads stick out their front doors,
Out their back doors flick their tails.
Belongings go along with them
No matter where they roam,
And you can visit anytime—
There's always someone home.

Skinks sneak
From cool crannies
To catnap in the sun,
Making themselves at home on slabs
Of stone.

In wintertime, coyotes hunt for jumpy prey,
Stippling the snowy slopes with tracks
Leading in and out of groves and glades,
Footprints left by loners, pairs, or packs.

Chins tipped up, they greet the chalky moon
And fill the sky with yips and howls and barks.
Bushy tails unfurl like silver plumes;
Watchful eyes glow golden in the dark.

Coyotes roam steep canyons face to face,
Ranging home terrain from peak to glen,
Crossing creek beds iced with frosty lace,
Spending restless days in borrowed dens.

Coyotes, jumpy prey, scan the plateau
For wolves and cougars hunting in the snow.

Strand by strand a spider strings
Her scaffold stalk to stem,
And when a passerby drops by
Midflight, she draws him in
Across the gauzy threshold
Into her homespun home.
He sticks around 'til dinnertime.
(She never eats alone.)

5

Snakes nest in secluded places—
Sandy strand to rocky scarp—
Depending on what snaky spaces
Suit the sorts of snakes they are.

Snakes that slide through sand and gravel,
Slither in a sizzling haze.
Other snakes that swim for travel
Squiggle through cool waterways.

Some seek desert scrub with sagebrush,
Cacti, mesquite, creosote.
Some reside in bankside rushes,
Marshy meadows, swampy moats.

Snug in burrows hidden under
Logs and tree stumps, stones and rocks,
Snakes stay safe from snow and thunder,
Snakes steer clear of hungry hawks.

Snakes nest in secluded places—
Sandy strand to rocky scarp—
Depending on what snaky spaces
Suit the sorts of snakes they are.

Grassland

The opening is small and round,
Leading steeply underground
Along a twisted passageway,
A route through roots from soil to clay.
At home within these dampish quarters,
Dim-eyed, furtive, furry boarders
Nibble on whatever squirms
(Like bugs) or slithers (such as worms).
A creature with a pointy snout
On occasion may pop out
To sniff a whiff of open sky
Or catch a breeze as it sails by—
A heady dose of heat and light
To take back to the world of night.

Hares carry on in hare-sized bowls,
In pairs or solitary.
They'd be amazed by rabbit holes—
A maze of tributaries—
And all the denizens and din
That occupy the space therein.
A warren is a riot—
Hares require quiet.

Hawks circle fields and furrows,
Slicing spirals in the sky.
Field mice scurry into burrows.
Hawks circle fields and furrows,
Keeping watch for shifting shadows,
Seeking spots where field mice hide.
Hawks circle fields and furrows,
Slicing spirals in the sky.

A critter skittles through a door
Between the baseboard and the floor
Into a space behind the wall—
A teeny, tiny place to crawl.
Tucked away, he frisks and fidgets,
Clicks his toenails, turns and twitches.
Crouched beside the crack to listen,
You can hear him switch position.
Late at night he gnaws and chatters,
To and fro he pitter-patters
With his mousie congregation,
Nibbling on the insulation.
   In the insides of the house
   There lives a mouse.

Shoreline

Shallow pools in rocky ledges,
Etched by sand and scored by sea,
Are beachfront homes for stranded creatures:
Starfish, snails, anemones.
Twice each day the sea seeps in
When the changing tide runs high.
Battered by the salty spray,
Sodden lodgers cling and sway,
Waterlogged before the drought,
Parching when the tide goes out.

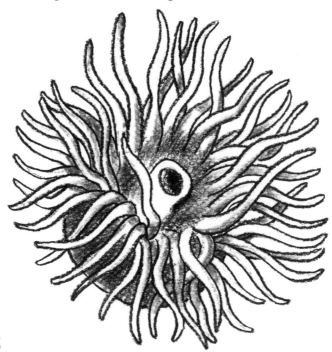

The hermit crab must somehow squeeze
His clampy claws and knobby knees
Into the bony folds of home,
A borrowed exoskeleton.

He tumbles with each tug of tide,
Curled in a curlicue inside
The twisted whorls of others' shells:
Periwinkles, whelks, or snails.

Tucked inside a tiny cloister
Once belonging to an oyster
Drill, he scrambles through the sand
Between the ocean and the land.

*O*tters loll like whiskered boats,
Bobbing gently in the swells.
Kelp beds help the otters float
While prying shellfish out of shells.
Thoughtful otters dot the ocean,
Heads awash with crabby notions.
What prey, tell, do otters dwell on?
Anything that has a shell on.

18

Salmon swim in river homes,
Under bridges, over stones,
Through cool pools in muted shadows,
Into sun-drenched, silver shallows.

Where the banks rise high and steep,
The water falls, the salmon leap.
Where the river stretches wide,
Salmon slowly drift and glide.

Salmon flash past hidden snags,
Skipping ripples, dodging crags.
Twirling, whirling, rushing free,
Swimming, homebound, from the sea.

Wetland

Herons walk with stilted steps,
Stalking, cautious, through the marsh,
Riffling the water's edge,
Proceeding in a stealthy march.
Each footfall kicks a cloudy plume,
A murky swirl of sediments,
Disturbing creatures in the gloom,
Unsettling their settlements.
Fish dart out of hiding places,
Flicker past the herons' knees,
Daring to seek safer spaces,
Deeper water, denser reeds.
Herons, filled with fishy bites, take flight,
For treetop colonies to spend the night.

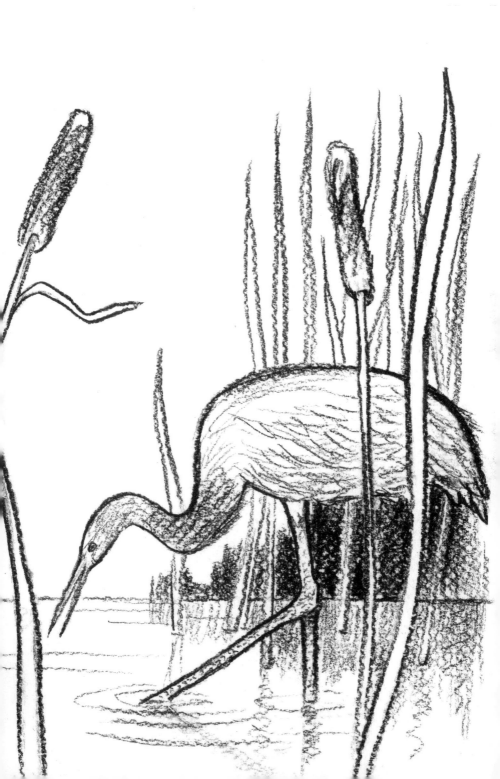

Ducks *Quack! Quack!* are careful when they choose
A marshy place *Quack! Quack!* to raise their broods,
Bankside where they *Quack! Quack! Quack!* can sip
Or nip or glide or splash *Quack! Quack!* or dip.
Proximity *Quack! Quack!* to water sources
Is, for ducks, of prime *Quack! Quack!* importance.
(Watching out *Quack! Quack!* for snapping turtles
Also *Quack! Quack! Quack! Quack!* never hurtles.)
What a life for *Quack! Quack!* happy ducklings,
Spending summer days *Quack! Quack! Quack!* dunking,
Hunting, smacking, snacking *Quack!* together,
Paddling like kayaks *Quack!* with feathers.
Come sundown *Quack! Quack!* in a downy rank,
Ducklings waddle *Quack! Quack!* up the bank.
Sleepy *Quack! Quack!* ducklings needing rest
Follow *Quack!* each other to their nest.

Some would find a beaver lodge quite cozy:
A loggy hut to house a colony,
A dreamy home for beavers feeling dozy.

Flowing channels lead to soggy quarters,
A bungalow below a clogged-up stream.
Some would find a beaver lodge quite cozy.

Saplings stuck together with a mortar
Made from mud, a silty recipe—
A dreamy home for beavers feeling dozy.

Eagerly incisors gnaw on timber,
Sticky bundles stashed for winter feasts.
Some would find a beaver lodge quite cozy.

Flat tails smack the surface of the water.
Nighttime swimmers find their dry retreat,
A dreamy home for beavers feeling dozy.

Morning sunbeams dancing on the river
Won't disturb the beavers, fast asleep.
Some would find a beaver lodge quite cozy.
A dreamy home for beavers feeling dozy.

Woodland

Bugs hunker
Under junk like
Rotting logs and
Flowerpots,
Buckets, baskets,
Bricks and shingles,
Garbage pails,
Flat stones, big rocks.

Bugs jam into
Gaps and fissures,
Slits in concrete,
Splits in trees,
Caulk the cracks
In walls and sidewalks,
Cling to under-
Sides of leaves.

Bugs bunk in
Garden bunkers,
Splintered posts and
Ruptured pipes,
Narrow breaches
Meant for creatures
Of a very
Tiny type.

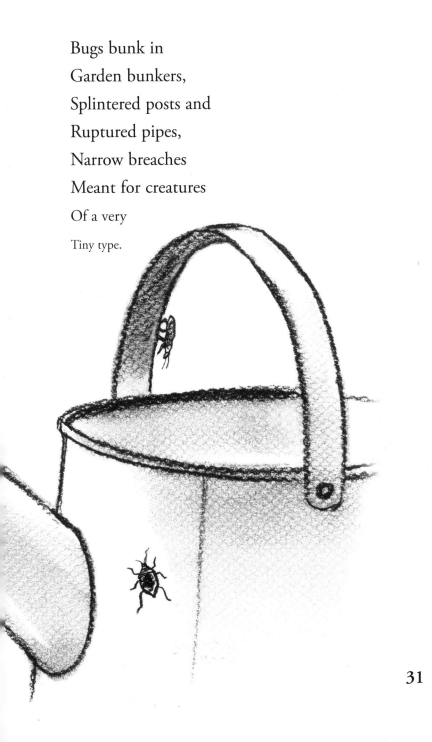

The sweetest home sweet home must be a hive,
Humming with activities of bees.
They never wipe their feet when they arrive;
They track their tacky nectar where they please.

When the workers' busy workday ends,
They take off in a beeline for the comb
To serve up royal jelly to their friends,
And get the latest buzz from all the drones.

Bears spend the wintertime slumbering snuggled,
With noses, ears, bellies, and paws in a huddle.
Bears wait for spring things, like berries and trout.
When springtime arrives, caved-in bears lumber out.

Wing-wrapped bats hang
Like fur bangles
In dank, dark caves.

A household tucked inside a hole
Or stuck inside a sticky bowl
Of twisted twigs and mud and stuff
Holds eggs or cheepy heaps of fluff
And various pairs of prickly feet,
Tiny feathers, pointy beaks.

Although it has a bird's-eye view,
With central air and skylights, too,
There's not a lot of room to grow.
Flighty families come and go.
As soon as one clan flies away,
Another mother comes to stay.

35

A doe will pick a thicket
As a place to place her fawn,
Its speckled hide well hidden
In the dappled forest lawn.
A bed safe in the shadows—
Mossy cushion, leafy crest—
A doe will pick a thicket
As a place to make a nest.

Habitats

The creatures featured in these poems make their homes in a variety of habitats, from sea to peak.

Desert
Desert habitats are characterized by poor soil and harsh conditions, making survival a challenge for plants and animals alike. Coyotes, skinks, snakes, tortoises, snails, and spiders rely on limited resources to survive shocking extremes of heat and drought.

Grassland
Grassland habitats are covered by grasses, dotted with only a few trees and shrubs. Imagine the prairie stretching to the horizon. Tall grasses sway in the breeze, turning from green to gold across the seasons. Mice, moles, and hares tunnel underground to find food and shelter; hawks circle overhead.

Shoreline
Shoreline habitats are located where the sea meets the land. At low tide, you can spot a world of creatures living in rocky spots that disappear as the sea

rises. Animals must adapt to every condition between soaking wet and bone dry. How do they stand up to crashing waves and lashing winds? Starfish and anemones lock onto rocks. Crabs burrow under the sand. Sea otters float just offshore.

Wetland

Wetland habitats stay flooded most of the time due to groundwater, river flow, tides, or rainwater. The water levels rise and fall with the seasons. Standing puddles in summer can grow into a swirling swamp once the rains begin. Long-legged birds wade through high water. Ducks waddle to nesting places. Turtles, snakes, beavers, fish, and other water-loving creatures hide in the reeds and rushes.

Woodland

Woodland habitats are large areas covered by a thick growth of trees and underbrush. Evergreens such as hemlocks, firs, cedars, and pines thrive high in the mountains. Broadleaf trees such as oaks and maples grow at lower elevations. Birds, bees, and bats make their homes in tree branches. Forest creatures such as deer and bears make their homes under shrubs and inside hollow logs.

Writing Poetry

As a writer, I'm often asked where I get my ideas, and I usually say that I poke my nose out the front door. I suggest you do the same. If you stay on the lookout for quirky, curious, and remarkable things, you'll soon discover them everywhere.

Most of the time when I sit down to write, I just sit down and write—but if I'm staring at a blank page, tackling a poetic form often gives me a push. For this book, I started out with a not very good poem about a hermit crab and worked my way out of a tight corner. Then I got to thinking about other homey places and made a list. It wasn't a bad beginning.

Tortoise (p. 2)

A homebody is someone who likes to stay home. In this poem, the unique physical characteristics of the creatures are expanded through wordplay to create a verse that is both funny and factual.

Skink (p. 3)

Five lines and twenty-two syllables make a cinquain:

Line 1—2 syllables
Line 2—4 syllables
Line 3—6 syllables
Line 4—8 syllables
Line 5—2 syllables

Coyote (p. 4)

This poem is a Shakespearean sonnet. It consists of three chunks, or stanzas, with four lines in each. At the end is a couplet (two lines that rhyme with each other) to make a comment or provide a punch line.

Line 1—a
Line 2—b
Line 3—a   rhymes with Line 1
Line 4—b   rhymes with Line 2

Line 5—c
Line 6—d
Line 7—c   rhymes with Line 5
Line 8—d   rhymes with Line 6

Line 9—e
Line 10—f
Line 11—e   rhymes with Line 9
Line 12—f   rhymes with Line 10

Line 13—g
Line 14—g   rhymes with Line 13

Spider (p. 5)

Remember what I said about poking your nose out the front door? The giant house spiders on my porch would inspire anyone. The final lines of this poem are an example of irony—what you think is going to happen heads off in a twisty direction.

Snake (pp. 6–7)

Sibilance refers to words that have the sound *s* or *sh*. Alliteration refers to words that begin with the same sound. Both help mimic the snakiness of snakes.

Mole (p. 10)

This poem is written in couplets, but it includes homophones and a few rhyming words tucked within the lines, too. (Homophones are words that sound alike but have different meanings and different spellings.) The similar vowel sounds in *route through roots* help make the tunnel even longer; *sniff a whiff* has just the nose-wiggly feeling I wanted to express.

Hare (p. 11)

Just because you are making stuff up doesn't mean that you don't need to do research. I did a lot of research for this book and found out all sorts of things I didn't know. For example, jackrabbits aren't rabbits at all: they are hares. Hares are similar to rabbits in a lot of ways, but they are bigger, for one thing, and they don't share rabbits' habits, as the poem points out.

Hawk (p. 12)

This form is called a triolet. It combines rhymes and repeated lines in a pattern that nicely matches the movement of a circling hawk:

Line 1—A
Line 2—B
Line 3—a   rhymes with Line 1
Line 4—A   repeats Line 1
Line 5—a   rhymes with Line 1
Line 6—b   rhymes with Line 2
Line 7—A   repeats Line 1
Line 8—B   repeats Line 2

Mouse (p. 13)

The fourteen lines let you know that this is a sonnet, but instead of following Shakespeare's rhyme scheme, this one has seven pairs of couplets.

Tidepool (p. 16)

For creatures in a tidepool, living conditions—either all wet or mostly dry—follow certain rules, but the transition period from one extreme to the other is marked by instability and chance. This poem follows a similar pattern. It begins at low tide with one rhyme scheme (ab cb), gets interrupted midway through when the tide comes in (an unrhymed couplet to suggest disorder), and ends at high tide with a different rhyme scheme (dd ee).

Hermit Crab (p. 17)

In this poem, I wanted to keep the language tightly packed to match how the crab fits itself into a shell. I used alliteration (*clampy claws*), assonance (repeated vowel sounds: *bony folds*), consonance (repeated ending consonants: *whorls, shells*), and repeated word parts (*curled, curlicue*) to make the sounds overlap just as the crab parts have to overlap.

Otter (p. 18)

Similes and metaphors can help you make comparisons that conjure up sharp images. This poem opens with a simile that compares an otter to a boat. If you've seen an otter, you know just what I mean. More important, if you haven't seen an otter, you know just what I mean.

Salmon (p. 19)

A list of razzle-dazzle words, along with a dictionary and a thesaurus, will help you create picture-perfect images and lively rhymes. For this poem, I picked through my collection of watery words to describe the changing course and character of the river as the salmon travel upstream.

Heron (pp. 22–23)

In this sonnet, I used alliteration to capture the awkwardness of stick-legged birds wading in a marsh, and contrasted their deliberate pace with the quickness of the fish running for cover.

Duck (pp. 24–25)

Onomatopoeia refers to sound words that mimic noises: *woof, chirp, screech, thud.* I was trying to write a duck poem and started using *Quack!* as a placeholder in lines that were too choppy. As I rewrote (and rewrote), the quacks stuck.

Beaver (pp. 26–27)

This form is called a villanelle. It has five three-line stanzas and one four-line stanza; lines from the first stanza repeat in an alternating pattern and then team up at the end. The rhyme scheme is supposed to repeat, too, but you'll see that I cheated a little bit (which is perfectly okay).

Stanza 1   Line 1—A1
            Line 2—b
            Line 3—A2   rhymes with Line 1

Stanza 2   Line 4—a   rhymes with Line 1
            Line 5—b   rhymes with Line 2
            Line 6—A1   repeats Line 1

Stanza 3   Line 7—a   rhymes with Line 1
            Line 8—b   rhymes with Line 2
            Line 9—A2   repeats Line 3

Stanza 4   same pattern as Stanza 2
Stanza 5   same pattern as Stanza 3

Stanza 6   Line 16—a   rhymes with Line 1
            Line 17—b   rhymes with Line 2
            Line 18—A1   repeats Line 1
            Line 19—A2   repeats Line 3

Bug (pp. 30–31)

Here, I brainstormed places that bugs live and then used the list to create the poem. The last lines, set in tiny type, are an example of a concrete poem, in which the text format matches the topic.

Bee (p. 32)

There are scads of examples of figurative language related to bees—a whole swarm of them—including alliteration, onomatopoeia, metaphor, slang, and wordplay.

Bear (p. 33)

Lines of poetry can be divided into groups of syllables called feet. Each foot follows a particular rhythmic pattern, or meter. This poem has four feet per line, and each foot has one strong syllable and two weak ones. The strong-weak-weak combination is called a dactyl, a waltz tempo that is very bearlike.

Bat (p. 34)

This Burmese form is called a than-bauk. It has three lines of four syllables each, with a built-in "climbing rhyme":

Line 1—4 syllables

Line 2—4 syllables; the third syllable rhymes with the fourth syllable in Line 1

Line 3—4 syllables; the second syllable rhymes with the third syllable in Line 2

I cheated a little bit in line 3 by leaning on assonance and ignoring the word ending, which bends the rule without completely breaking it.

Bird (p. 35)

I wrote this poem as a kind of real estate ad, describing the nest at a rompy pace to match the flap and chatter of the birds that use it.

Deer (pp. 36–37)

For this poem I chose words and phrases that stress the need for secrecy and seclusion. The sharp-edged internal rhyme of the first and last lines protects the softer sibilance of the poem's interior lines. The homonyms and their related words add rhythm and an extra layer to the text that matches the idea of keeping the fawn tucked out of view.

Acknowledgments

To the poets, teachers, mentors, friends, and family members who offered encouragement, support, generous praise, and insightful criticism, thank you, thank you, thank you: Nancy Andersen, Carmen T. Bernier-Grand, Susan Colburn, Carolyn Conahan, Chris Coughlin, Betty Cramer, Charlene DeLage, Nancy Devine, Heather Frederick, Gina Hietpas, Loretta Johnson, Hope Kingsley, Ursula LeGuin and the Coyotes, Bernice Lincoln, Deb Lund, Emily Mitchell, Rosanne Parry, Ann Whitford Paul, Chris Reynolds, Ann Teplick, Barb Tracer, Nancy Tune, Meredith Mundy Wasinger, Alison Wells, Emily Whitman, Lauren Williams, Linda Zuckerman, and especially Mrs. Nichols, Grade 3, Room 6, Green Gables Elementary School, Palo Alto, California, 1961.

For Dad, Jeff, and *mi hijita*, Rudy,
with love—S. B.

For my beloved critters,
Marty and Daisy—J. H.

Text copyright © 2010 by Susan Blackaby
Illustrations copyright © 2010 by Jamie Hogan

Published by Charlesbridge
85 Main Street
Watertown, MA 02472
(617) 926-0329
www.charlesbridge.com

Library of Congress Cataloging-in-Publication Data
Blackaby, Susan.
    Nest, nook & cranny / Susan Blackaby ; illustrated by Jamie Hogan
        p. cm.
    ISBN 978-1-58089-350-3 (reinforced for library use)
1. Habitat (Ecology)—Juvenile literature. I. Hogan, Jamie, ill. II.
Title. III. Title: Nest, nook, and cranny.
QH541.14.B58 2010
577—dc22   2009004302

Printed in China
(hc) 10 9 8 7 6 5 4 3 2 1

Illustrations done in pastel and charcoal pencil on Canson paper
Display type and text type set in Sketchley and Adobe Garamond Pro
Color separations by Chroma Graphics, Singapore
Printed and bound September 2009 by Jade Productions
    in ShenZhen, Guangdong, China
Production supervision by Brian G. Walker
Designed by Whitney Leader-Picone